About the Author

The visas stamped on the passport of CHARLES JOY — Boston-born, Phi Beta Kappa, *cum laude,* Harvard graduate— have expanded to World Almanac proportions. A frontier official in Nyasaland, checking that passport, remarked: "You aren't home much, are you?" "Yes," was the reply, for Dr. Joy has been "at home" for two decades in 120 countries of the world, most recently in Israel.

Prior to assignment with World War II and Korean war relief agencies, including CARE and SAVE THE CHILDREN FEDERATION, he held seven successive church pastorates. He has been decorated by five foreign governments for his work with children and is an officer of the French Academy. His twenty books include three in Coward-McCann's *Challenge* series.

About the Illustrator

Dayton Art Institute graduate KATHLEEN ELGIN has illustrated twenty children's books. When not at work in her year-round Fire Island home, where she braves blizzards as well as hurricanes, her favorite pastime is a painting spree abroad. Borgard, her dachshund, is named for the German car Miss Elgin used while capturing the Rhine on canvas. Both Borgard and the Elgin brush have been intrigued by faces and places, the world over.

Getting to Know
Israel

*Getting to know*_____

ISRAEL

CHARLES R. JOY

illustrated by KATHLEEN ELGIN

COWARD·McCANN · NEW YORK

Author, illustrator, and publisher wish to acknowledge with appreciation the courtesy and technical assistance given by Miss Lillian Baral of the Israel Government Tourist Office, Mr. Shmuel Gerstman and Mr. Meir Padan of the Israel Office of Information, who checked the manuscript for accuracy of fact and interpretation and made invaluable suggestions.

Library of Congress Catalog Card Number: 60-5680

MANUFACTURED IN THE UNITED STATES OF AMERICA

Editor of this Series: Sabra Holbrook

Second Impression

One of the railways in Israel runs so close to the border of Jordan that once a conductor walked through the cars crying out, "Ladies and gentlemen, please don't stick your heads out of the country." Israel is a little bit of a country, only about the size of Massachusetts. At its narrowest point, you can walk across it in a day.

Mediterranean
Sea

Haifa
+ Mt.
Carmel

Sea
of
Galilee
Nazareth

Jordan River

Tel Aviv
Yafo

Jerusalem
Mt. Zion

Dead
Sea

ISRAEL

NEGEV

Eilat

Red Sea

TURKEY
PERSIA
LEBANON
SYRIA
GAZA STRIP
JORDAN
IRAQ
EGYPT
SAUDI ARABIA

6

This little land is enclosed by Lebanon on the north and Jordan on the east, the Syrian part of the United Arab Republic on the northeast, and the Egyptian part on the south. On the southwest is the Gaza strip, claimed by both Israel and the Egyptian state. Egyptians occupy Gaza. At its southernmost end, Israel comes to a sharp point on the shore of the Red Sea. The blue waves of the Mediterranean break on Israel's west coast.

The Mediterranean is its only friendly neighbor. On land, it is completely surrounded by enemies. But enemies are nothing new to Israel. All through history, it has been the field of bloody battles.

Its position in the Middle East makes it a bridge between continents. It's an Asiatic country that lies close to both Europe and Africa. In the old days, great caravan routes crossed it. Traders with laden camels, soldiers with shields and spears, kings and emperors invaded it from all sides. Even children once tried to invade it.

This land was such a center of attention that it is no wonder map makers of the Middle Ages put it in the center of the world. They called it Palestine, which was the name the Romans gave it when they ruled the land. The Romans were neither its first nor its last conquerors. Before them were the Assyrians, Babylonians, Persians, and Macedonians. After them came Arabs, Tartars, and Crusaders.

The Crusaders were Christians from western Europe who felt it was their duty to win back from non-Christians the Holy Land where Jesus had lived. There were seven crusades in all. One was made up of 50,000 French and German children. The children never reached the Holy Land. Some of the grown-up Crusaders didn't either. However, Crusaders finally established a Christian kingdom in Jerusalem, the capital of Palestine. But then the Turks drove them out of the land.

The rule of the Turks ended with the First World War. The League of Nations asked Great Britain to take charge of Palestine. During the years Great Britain was in charge, followers of Judaism were encouraged to return to the land where their religion was born. Judaism is the name of the Hebrew religion. But still, they could not call the land their own. It hadn't been wholly theirs since 600 years before the birth of Jesus.

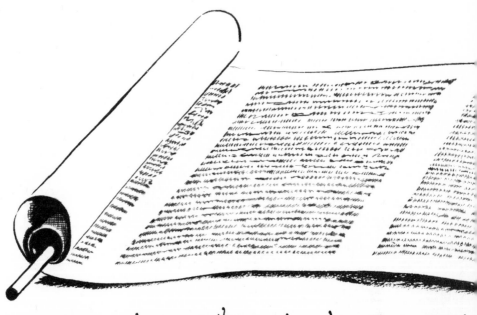

שְׁמַע יִשְׂרָאֵל יְהֹוָה אֱלֹהֵינוּ יְהֹוָה ׀ אֶחָד׃

In ancient times, the Hebrews had been enslaved by the Egyptians. To get back home, they hiked 40 years through the desert, with their Egyptian masters chasing them part of the way. You can read the exciting story of their escape in the Old Testament of the Bible. The first five books of this testament contain the basic laws of Judaism. Jewish worshipers call these books the Torah.

In later books, the Old Testament tells how the Hebrews were captured again. After they escaped from Egypt, they lived in their native land for 1,000 years. Then the Babylonians conquered the southern half of the country and took the people away as captives. The Assyrians conquered the northern half and its people disappeared. Historians call them "the lost tribes," because no one knows what happened to them.

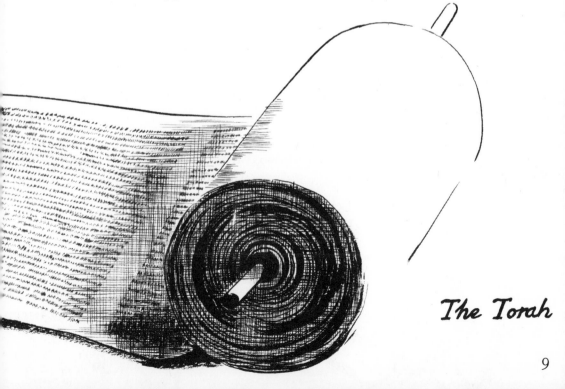

The Torah

In the long generations while Israel was ruled by others, many believers in Judaism became citizens of the various countries in which they settled. For centuries, they were respected members of their communities. Countries like the United States and other democracies became their homes. Most of their descendants think of modern Israel as a brave new land, but not as *their* land. Their homes are where they live now.

But there were also countries, especially those ruled by dictators, where Jews were not made to feel at home. They had to practice their religion in secret. Sometimes they were murdered by the hundreds and thousands.

To these Jews, May 14, 1948, was a holy day. It was the new Israel's birthday. The United Nations had decided to divide the territory the British had been watching over into two independent states, one Jewish, the other Arab. The Jewish state became the Republic of Israel.

Those Israelis who had already come home while the British were in charge danced and sang in the streets. Their eyes were shining with joy.

The next day their laughter turned to tears. Bombs dropped in the streets where they had been dancing. The Arab nations were attacking them. There were more Arabs than Jews in Israel. They had been living there for many centuries. They had their own religion, their own ways. The Arab peoples in neighboring countries felt that Israel belonged to the Arabs who had been living there so long. These countries sent their planes over Israel, their tanks and troops across its borders.

To the surprise of the world, the Israelis defeated the Arab armies and drove them out of the land. Israel signed armistices with the Arab attackers. But there is no real peace to this day. All the borders are guarded by the Israelis on their side and the Arabs on theirs. Battles often break out between them.

Both men and women serve in the army of Israel, and both men and women work side by side to build the farms, cities, and industries of this new country. There are 2 million Israelis and they come from 70 nations. They are all colors and kinds. There are white Israelis, black Israelis, yellow Israelis. There are brunettes and blondes. There are redheads with freckles.

We call the United States a melting pot because so many different nationalities came to make contributions in our land. If the United States is a melting pot, then Israel must be a pressure cooker, people say. During the first four years of Israel's independence, its population doubled.

About half the first immigrants came from Europe. They escaped from Hitler's Nazis, as the dictator and his soldiers took over country after country. The Nazis persecuted all religious groups, but especially those of Jewish faith. The newcomers today are from India and China, Ethiopia and Morocco, Tunisia and Afghanistan, and other parts of Asia, Africa, and the Middle East. A few come from the United States.

Yemenite
Basket Maker

14

In some cases practically all the Jewish people of a particular country have come to Israel. The Yemenite Jews are an example. The Jews had known little but misery in Yemen. Only at night could they leave the crowded neighborhoods, called "ghettos," where they were forced to live, apart from other people. Wherever they went, they were made to go barefoot. At last they were permitted to leave the land. They walked hundreds of miles to British Aden. There, big C-54 Skymasters picked them up. The big planes flew them to freedom in Israel. The flight was called Operation Magic Carpet. The American Jewish Joint Distribution Committee helped the Israel government pay for it.

Almost all the Jews from Iraq came to Israel also. One hundred twenty-six thousand of them took the train to Baghdad, the capital of Iraq. Then planes picked them up. These planes, too, were sent with aid from American Jews. The airlift from Baghdad to Iraq was called Operation Ali Baba — after a character in the Arabian Nights. To most of the people, these planes were as miraculous as those old tales.

Hardly any of the passengers, however, had ever flown before. They were excited, but they were also afraid. They were especially alarmed when they were tied to their seats. At the last moment some of them stayed behind.

The government sends these homecomers from Yemen, Iraq, and scores of other lands to settlements where work is waiting for them. They may settle down in a green valley, a brown desert, or a big city. Those who are farmers may have to help make their own farmland from the desert. They may hope some day to make their homes in the long plain that runs along the edge of the Mediterranean Sea. It is fertile and well watered and the best farms are there.

To the east of the plain the land rises to hills, then to mountains, 3,000 to 4,000 feet high. Beyond the mountains the land falls sharply to the valley of the Jordan River, in which Jesus was baptized. The river valley is the deepest on the surface of the earth.

The Jordan rises in the mountains of the north, then flows down

into the Sea of Galilee, on the shores of which Jesus preached. To-day, as in that time, fishermen still cast their nets and women bearing pitchers on their heads gather around the village wells to gossip. The sea is harp-shaped and sometimes it is called Kinereth — which means "Lake of the Harp" in Hebrew.

From the Galilean Sea, the Jordan flows down to the Dead Sea. Set in a rift between two mountain ranges, the Dead Sea is the lowest spot on the whole globe. It is almost 1,300 feet below the level of the ocean. Surrounded by limestone cliffs that look like bleak crags of the moon, the Dead Sea glistens serene and deep blue in the hot sun. The water is so salty that no one can sink in it. It is five times as salty as the Atlantic Ocean. Most visitors want to take a dip for the fun of it. If they aren't careful, the brine stings their eyes. Not many want to go in a second time.

Carnalite extracted from the Dead Sea

There are three reasons for the saltiness. First, small streams that flow into it have absorbed salt buried in the soil through which they flow. Second, there are salty hot springs on the sea bottom. The third reason is the hot sun. It evaporates the moisture constantly, leaving the salt.

There are other minerals in the Dead Sea, too. The most important one is carnalite. From the carnalite, potash is extracted. It is a chemical used in making fertilizers. It is also used to make bombs. There is a big potash plant at the southern end of the Dead Sea. Potash is one of Israel's biggest exports.

Below the Dead Sea is a triangular desert called the Negev. The word means "south" in Hebrew. The Negev is very much like our Wild West in America. The little towns have wide, dusty streets lined with rude buildings. Cowboys herd cattle on vast ranches. Everywhere prospectors are at work. They are looking for water and minerals. Sometimes they are hunting oil. They have already found several good wells. The men wear jeans or shorts, khaki shirts, and boots or sandals. They are often thirsty, always hot, and their clothes are dusty with sand.

The Negev is full of sand. The people that live there are full of grit. It takes courage to try to turn a dry desert into a fruitful land.

At the very tip end of the Negev, where Israel comes to a point on a gulf of the Red Sea, are the fabled mines where King Solomon found all his copper. Israelis still mine copper there. The copper and other goods are shipped out from Eilat, a new port on the gulf. The Red Sea waters are warm all year round, and children from the Negev like to skin dive in them, hunting for shells and watching the bright-colored fish.

King Solomon's mines

There is little rain in the Negev at any time of the year. There is very little in the rest of Israel, either, from April to November. During these months, the sun is bright, the skies cloudless. The Israelis are fond of fun and they joke about the dry weather. One of their newspapers once printed this story: A drop of water fell on a man and knocked him unconscious — so they threw two pails of dust on him to revive him!

In the spring and the fall a hot wind often blows over Israel. If you have ever stood in front of an open furnace door you know what that wind feels like. It's called the *khamsin* and sometimes it's filled with desert dust that reminds you of furnace ashes.

In the winter there is plenty of rain — often far too much. The people are trying to store this rain in reservoirs so they will have it to water the land when no rain falls.

If you were to visit this little country of rivers and plains and lakes and mountains and deserts, you could choose your means of travel from a dozen different international lines. You might choose the fine new steamship *Jerusalem* of the Israel Zim Line. From the east coast of the United States it takes two weeks to reach the city of Haifa by boat. Or you might travel by the Israel airline, El Al. The flight takes less than a day. It lands you at the Lod Airport near the big city of Tel-Aviv. "Blessed be ye who come," is the greeting of the airline's ground hostess. You have touched the soil of Israel.

Most of the people who come to live in Israel arrive by ship at Haifa. They are so happy to be there that Haifa is called "the point of first joy."

Haifa is one of Israel's three great cities, and its largest port. It is a busy manufacturing center. A pipeline brings oil to the city all the way from the Red Sea. Refineries in Haifa purify the oil. Other factories make soap and cement, glass and textiles.

The city has iron foundries and a big automobile assembly plant.

Haifa Bay
and Haifa, seen from Mt. Carmel

It has a huge fertilizer and chemical plant. This plant uses nitrogen, which it gets from the air. It uses phosphates, which it gets from mines in the Negev. It uses potash, which it gets from the Dead Sea. The fertilizer is not only used in Israel but is sent to countries in Africa and Asia to help them modernize their farming.

Israelis call Haifa a "cake of three layers." The wharves and factories are the bottom layer close to the bay. Back of the waterfront rises beautiful Mount Carmel. On its slopes are a second layer of business houses, city buildings, hotels. There are woodsy parks, too, but there are no KEEP OFF THE GRASS signs. By a goldfish pond there is a sign, however, which shows two fish. It reads, *Dear children, don't give us any food. We have plenty, and more would hurt us.*

On the summit of Mount Carmel are airy villas, where people

live. The Israelis call this mountain the Vineyard of God. It was here, in Old Testament days, that the prophet Elijah challenged the prophets of the heathen god Baal. Elijah called fire down from heaven to kindle the water-soaked wood of his altar. The prophets of Baal couldn't do this. The people became followers of the Hebrew God.

Haifa is a proud and lovely city, but it is not Israel's largest. Tel-Aviv is. Fifty years ago Tel-Aviv didn't exist. Then people began to build houses on great sand dunes along the shores of the Mediterranean, north of an ancient fishing village called Jaffa. The dune town grew so big that it swallowed up Jaffa, which is now called Yafo.

Tel-Aviv

Yafo has kept its narrow cobbled alleyways, but Tel-Aviv is a city of broad boulevards. The streets are lined with flat-roofed apartment houses, modern office buildings, and bright sidewalk cafés. More than 300,000 people make Tel-Aviv a bustling place, the headquarters of most of Israel's commerce. Here, too, in this city, whose name means "Hill of Spring," are museums, theatres, opera. It is a center of art as well as commerce.

Only 40 miles from Tel-Aviv is Israel's third largest city. This is the historic capital, Jerusalem. There is a shuttle taxi running between Tel-Aviv and Jerusalem. It's called a *sherut*, and it is very convenient.

The ride to Jerusalem is exciting. There is so much to see on the way. Near the coast are great groves of oranges, lemons, grape-fruit, and tangerines. Israel sells these to other nations. There are olive groves and fig orchards, dairy and poultry farms. Patches of color glow where people grow flowers to be sold in the flower shops. Many of the houses are gay with the red-blossomed, thorny-stemmed bougainvillaea.

If you are one of the six passengers in the sherut, you exclaim at the many kinds of wild flowers, too. You start naming them: red anemones, blue lupines, daisies, poppies, iris, and jonquils.

The paved road you travel on is called the Road of Courage. It was built during the war with the Arabs, which Israelis call the War of Independence. Over the Road of Courage, by night, brave men carried supplies to the people of Jerusalem. They delivered their loads right under the noses and the guns of the enemy.

The road winds upward among the hills. The forests here are not yet very tall, but they are growing fast. Formerly the people cut down the trees to make charcoal. They let their goats eat the seedlings. Most of the old trees disappeared and no new ones grew. Now the government encourages all the people to plant new trees.

In the United States and other foreign lands people give money for trees in Israel. There are many baby pine trees now, cedars and eucalyptus, carobs also. The carobs bear long brown pods with a sweetish pulp inside. Animals like to eat the pods — people eat them too, sometimes. Children love to help plant all the different kinds of trees. School classes plant and tend their own. Many trees along the Road of Courage were planted to honor the heroes who fought and died to keep Israel's freedom.

In other parts of Israel, other kinds of trees and plants are grown. In the hot Jordan Valley people grow date palms and bananas. All over Israel the cactus grows by itself. The cactus with its sharp spines makes a wonderful hedge. It keeps animals where they belong.

You see many animals as you climb the Road of Courage, donkeys and asses, cattle and goats, perhaps camels. You may see wild animals too: deer and gazelles, foxes and rabbits. When you reach Jerusalem you will almost certainly hear the shrill howling of the jackals after ten in the evening. People call them "Jerusalem dogs." The howling does not make those who keep hens happy. Jerusalem dogs seem to like chicken dinners as much as you do. They like them in the rough, too.

To Israelis, Jerusalem is a holy city, the spiritual center of the country. As you see its domes and towers rising above you, it seems a golden city. The buildings are mostly yellow stone — not strange in a land where wood is so precious and stone so plentiful.

To your surprise you find that Jerusalem is not one city but two. The oldest part is believed to be 5,000 years old. During the war, the Arabs seized most of the old Jerusalem. It is now under the rule of the Kingdom of Jordan. The Israel section is bright with modern government buildings, good shops, and hotels. But some of its quarters are as strange as if they were in another world.

Narrow alleys and stairways wind through crowded bazaars where spice, butter, oil, and golden trinkets are sold. Everything is carefully wrapped in brown paper. There are no open displays. The merchant gladly unwraps his wares for any customer who asks to see them. After a cup of coffee, bargaining starts. A good bargainer makes his purchase for half the price that's asked. Both the merchant and the customer enjoy the argument.

Some of the merchants' shops are squeezed between old synagogues. A synagogue is a Jewish house of worship. Entering it are men with silk coats, long black socks, mink hats, and hair that curls around their ears. They are the men of Poland. Women with long cotton skirts, little flowered caps, and white woolen shawls are shopping in the bazaars. The women have come from the mountains of Asiatic Russia.

A man walks by, wearing an embroidered cap and white caftan. His caftan is a robe which he has gathered at his waist with a rope-like belt. His hands are hidden by long sleeves. He comes from the distant country of Bokhara. He pushes his way past loaded donkeys and small herds of goats and sheep being driven to slaughter.

By mistake, he bumps into a group of men in baggy white pants, and black and white-striped coats. Scarves are wound around their close-cropped hair. Several of the men have black mustaches. They are Arabs.

And here comes a girl in a short dress with a sunback. She is swinging hands with a boy in shorts. She wears sandals, he a pair of sneakers. These young folk are dressed sensibly for the climate.

On the highest hill in this part of Jerusalem, under a great stone slab, lies the body of the man who spent his life working to make Israel a homeland for all these different kinds of people.

His name was Theodore Herzl. He was the father of Zionism. This name was chosen for his work because in the Old Testament the word "Zion" is often used to mean paradise. There is a Mount Zion in Jerusalem and the Old Testament sometimes calls the whole city by that name. The ancient Hebrews and some of the early founders of the Christian church described paradise as an even lovelier Jerusalem — or Zion.

Zionism's founder died in Vienna, but more than fifty years later his body was brought to Jerusalem. Crowds of people threw little bags of earth from all parts of the country into his grave. Theodore Herzl had come home.

On Mount Zion, close to the Jordan-Israel boundary, there is an ancient fortress. Here the shepherd boy David, who defeated the giant Goliath and became king of Israel, is supposed to rest. Mount Zion shadows the house where it is said that Jesus and the disciples ate supper together for the last time.

Reminders of the Bible are everywhere in Jerusalem — even in the zoo. It is called the Biblical Zoo and it contains many of the animals and plants mentioned in the Bible. Each exhibit has a sign quoting the Bible verse which mentions it.

A LION WHICH IS STRONGEST AMONG BEASTS + TURNETH NOT AWAY FOR ANY

From the high tower of the Young Men's Christian Association you can look over the walls that divide the Jordan and Israel sections of the city. Although the "Y" is called "Christian," 95 per cent of its members are of Jewish faith.

From the tower you will see the Mount of Olives, with the garden of Gethsemane, where Jesus prayed the night before the Crucifixion.

You want to visit it of course.

But look out! That's not easy. And you may not return.

At the foot of the old walls is a no man's land, tangled over with barbed wire. Soldiers with rifles watch everyone who comes close.

There is a way through the barbed wire that leads to the Mandelbaum Gate between the two sections of the city. At the gate more armed soldiers stand.

If your religion is Judaism, the soldiers will not let you pass. If you are Christian, only at Christmas and Easter can you go through and return. Other times of year, you can pass, but you cannot come back.

Those who get through can see many famous places, sacred to Christian, Mohammedan, and Jew. There is the enclosure where once King Solomon's temple stood. It was built of cedar and stone and gold and jewels. Later, Moslems built a dome in the enclosure. Under the dome is a great ledge. Here, Moslem tradition says that God began to create the world. The Moslems also say that the ledge is the spot from which Mohammed went up to Heaven on a white, winged horse. You can see big fingerprints in the rock. Moslems say these were made when the angel Gabriel pressed down with his hand to keep the rock from flying right up into heaven after the prophet. The Moslems believe in angels, and Gabriel is the chief of them.

Also in the Jordan section is the Via Dolorosa, the road over which Jesus stumbled on the way to the Crucifixion. The Church of the Holy Sepulchre is the place where many think Jesus was buried.

High on Mount Scopus in old Jerusalem is a ghost university. Its corridors are still, its classrooms deserted. When the city was divided, Israelis could no longer attend the Hebrew University on the Jordan side. They built a magnificent new one in a suburb of Jerusalem. It looks a little like the United Nations buildings — with many windows in the walls. Between classes, students can study in gardens and patios.

The new Hebrew University is the home of some of the world's oldest treasures. The treasures were discovered by some Arab boys who were tending goats in the desert land around the Dead Sea.

One of their goats hid in a hole among the rocks. A boy threw a stone in to make the goat come out. He heard something inside break, something that sounded like a dish. The next day he went back and crawled into what turned out to be a cave. To his surprise he found earthenware jars containing rolls of leather. There was writing on the rolls, old Hebrew writing.

and the first century after Jesus' death. They were the earliest biblical writings man had ever found. You could look at them! You could touch them!

There is a lot of buried history in this part of the world.

When you visit Israel you are walking in the footsteps of people who lived a great many years ago. The Bible says that a thousand years in God's sight are like only yesterday. The Dead Sea Scrolls take you back 2,000 years. But that's nothing. Just the day before yesterday! Up near the Sea of Galilee, archaeologists have found axes that are 100,000 years old.

But history isn't just the story of olden times. The little country of Israel is also making history today — maybe in a big way. The writers of Israel's modern history are pioneers. They may be manufacturers, or engineers, or teachers, or miners, or artists, or scientists, or sailors. Whatever they are, they are building a new country.

Many of those who come to Israel are graduates of universities. They have been lawyers and professors and writers. They have degrees, such as doctor of philosophy, doctor of literature, doctor of law, or doctor of medicine. Yet some of them take the humblest of jobs. They want to.

Israelis tell a story about a line of men passing bricks for a new building from hand to hand. They are saying to one another: "Please, doctor," and "Thank you, doctor."

For many of the newcomers the life is rugged. The great plain of

Fragment of a Scroll

central Israel, called the Emek, was once mostly marshland. The marshes produced a fine crop of mosquitoes, but nothing else. The mosquitoes spread malaria, and many of the pioneers died of it. Then the people dug ditches and drained off the water. Now the Emek is fertile. It is dotted with little villages where people live in tree-shaded homes.

There was a low, marshy lake in the north called Lake Huleh. If you go looking for it today you won't find it. The pioneers drained it by digging a deeper channel for the Jordan River that flows through it. Now cotton, rice, and sugar beets grow where once the marsh reeds and mosquitoes reigned.

Many of the pioneers went down to the Negev desert. In some parts of the desert near the Dead Sea, the soil is at least 20 per cent salt. Pioneers began to wash the earth. They built mud dikes around their fields, and covered the land with fresh water from the River Jordan, which is less than a mile away. The water soaked into the earth and carried the salt down with it. When the soil had been washed about ten times, there was no salt left within five or six feet of the surface. Then the land needed fertilizer, so the people put fish into the shallow ponds. After a few months the fish had left a coating of organic fertilizer on the bottom. Then the ponds were drained. Now the people grow garden vegetables and bananas in the fresh, fertilized soil.

Only a nation young in spirit would attempt such tasks as these.
Modern Israelis are changing the face of an old land.

Children who come from other lands to live in Israel begin to be proud of the new state as soon as they arrive. In schools, they study its history and geography. Some also have to learn very simple things: how to feed chickens, how to plant a garden, and how to make a bed. All of them study Hebrew.

There is good reason for the study of Hebrew.

Just imagine that the pupils in your class speak nothing but the Malabar dialect of Hindustani. A teacher in one village in the Negev had such a class. Or suppose there are children from seventeen countries in your class, speaking seventeen different languages. Some are Europeans, some are from North Africa, and some from the Middle East. You discover that a number of your classmates have never eaten with a knife and fork, never slept in a bed, never seen a book. They speak only about a hundred words. They can't write their own names.

How will a teacher help build a united nation from classes like these? First, she must teach a common language.

At the very beginning the Israel government had to decide what the common language was to be. Although they chose Hebrew as the official language, they decided to have Arabic as a second one, because there were so many Arabs in the land.

As for the Jews who came back to Israel, almost everyone knew a little Hebrew. It had been the language of the Old Testament, the language of the prophets, the language of the land when it belonged to the Hebrews. Most newcomers knew at least the Hebrew prayers. A good many knew Yiddish, which is a mixture of German and Hebrew. Others knew Ladino, which is a mixture of Spanish and Hebrew.

Still, a language that was alive 2,000 years ago would hardly do for today. The old Hebrew, of course, had no words for carburetor, television, electronics, baseball, polio, fountain pen. There were no words for thousands upon thousands of things that are common today. New words had to be found. Some were taken over from other languages. Sport, garage, autobus, baby sitter and *puntcher* (puncture) came from us. You don't need to guess what a *sandvich* and a *svetter* are.

A *jip* is a jeep, which goes everywhere in Israel. This jip has a *beck-ex,* or back axle. It also has a front beck-ex, or front axle. As you ride along in your jip you will see many *trempestim.* Trempestim are hitchhikers. The word comes from our word "tramp."

There is a lot of *sleng* (slang) in Israel today. The word *artiste* comes from the French. In Israel it means a man who never does any work. People say there are two kinds of men in the army, soldiers and artistes. *Nylon* is sleng for "terrific." *Eisen,* the German word for iron, is sleng for "colossal."

The written language is very different from ours. The first letter of the alphabet is *alef,* which is written א . The second letter is *beit,* which is written ב . The word for alphabet is *alef-beit.* You begin reading a Hebrew book at what we would call the last page. Every line is read from right to left, not from left to right, as we read.

Education is now compulsory in Israel. Boys and girls have to go to school for nine years, from the time they are five until they are fourteen. If they don't get good enough marks to graduate from elementary school when they are fourteen, they have to stay until they do, or until they are eighteen.

There are more than half a million students and not nearly enough school buildings. In the country, classes are sometimes held

in tents, with pupils squatting on the ground. In the city, there are sometimes two shifts. But Israel is building schools as fast as possible. The new ones are made of concrete and glass, surrounded by lawns and flowers. You would enjoy studying in them.

After the elementary grades, boys and girls may go on to high school, then a university, or technical school. These schools are not compulsory nor free, but they don't charge much.

It is not only the children, however, who have to be educated. A great many grownups need some schooling too. They go to the *ulpanim,* or academies, which charge a small fee. Ulpanim hold classes both day and night. Night classes are for those who work during the day.

The workers who are building the new state live in all kinds of shelters: tents, aluminum huts, prefabs, wooden, concrete, and stone houses.

Some of them live in *kibbutzim. Kibbutzim* is the plural of *kibbutz,* which means a settlement where everyone shares alike. Nobody gets any pay for his work. But the kibbutz promises to take care of all its members until they die. On farm kibbutzim, children work, too. They raise chickens and tend gardens.

There are kibbutzim of different kinds all over Israel. The oldest of them is Daganya Alef. *Daganya* means cornflower. Beside this kibbutz there is another called Daganya Beit. These two kibbutzim, Cornflower A, and Cornflower B, are farms. They are at the southern end of the Sea of Galilee just where the Jordan River flows out of it.

It is very hot there, for the sea is 650 feet below the level of the ocean. But the waters of the Jordan are cold and clear. The children of the two kibbutzim can always cool off by diving into the river. The Jordan is deep here and the current is swift. It takes strength to swim upstream. But it's lots of fun.

On these kibbutzim, the people grow bananas and grapefruit, clover, alfalfa, and other crops. They have thousands of hens and big herds of cows. They milk the cows by electricity.

The mothers put all their babies into a nursery. Then they come every day to feed them and to put them to sleep. When the babies are two years old, they go to live with their parents. When the boys and girls are fourteen, they go to a home for young people. In the home, each boy or girl has two or three roommates.

All the babies born in a kibbutz are *sabras*. A sabra is someone born in Israel, instead of having come from another country. A whole generation of these young Israeli makes up about one third of the population. They are strong and healthy, brought up on sunshine, orange juice, and hard work. They are proud, independent, fine youngsters.

Sabra is a good name for them. In Hebrew, it means "cactus." The flower of the cactus is very beautiful. The fruit is prickly on the outside, but very sweet inside. When the sabras, both young men and young women, were fighting against the Arabs on the dangerous frontiers of Israel, the people used to say: "Our sabras are afraid of nothing — except their mothers."

Of course, not all the people that come to Israel enter kibbutzim. People are free to choose their work.

Many who are working to build the new state think they are fulfilling ancient prophecies about the revival of the land. They are devoted to the religion of the Hebrew people. Their very names, David, Solomon, Abraham, Jacob, Leah, Rachel, Sarah, are often taken from the Old Testament.

Some of the younger people don't take the laws of Judaism as seriously as their elders do. There are many of these laws about ways to prepare food, to clean house, to slaughter animals, to behave on holy days. There are also laws about how to do business and bring up children. You can read them in the books of Exodus, Leviticus, Numbers, and Deuteronomy in the Bible.

You can read the Ten Commandments in the Book of Exodus. All Jews accept these laws, regardless of whether they practice the others. They believe in love of God and neighbor. Judaism was the first religion in the world to teach belief in one God.

Both Christianity and Mohammedanism are based on Judaism. This is one of the reasons everybody should know about Judaism. Jesus was a Jew. Mohammed honored the old Hebrew prophets.

There are some Christians in Israel today, but there are about three times as many Mohammedans, or Moslems. Most of the Arabs are Moslems, and there are over 150,000 of them. Unlike most of their people, they did not flee when the Israel-Arab War broke out.

Five times a day, the *muezzin,* who is the Moslem crier, calls the faithful to prayer from the minarets, or tall towers, that rise above their mosques. Then the Arabs turn their faces toward Mecca, their holy city. Wherever they may be, when the muezzin calls, they pray. On Friday they go to the mosque and think about the prophet Mohammed, and the teaching he left them in their holy book, the Koran.

The Bedouins are Moslems too. About 20,000 of them wander around in the Negev, living in black, goatskin tents. The Bedouins hate farming. They depend on their herds of camels, their flocks of sheep and goats. Now the changing times are forcing many into agriculture. It is hard work, and the Bedouins don't like it at first, but almost everybody works hard in Israel. Probably nowhere else in the world do people work harder.

Hard work hasn't killed their sense of fun. On the contrary, rugged pioneering makes play even more important. They play as hard as they work. They joke and laugh, sing, shout, and dance. They have a gift for gaiety. They are a joyous, sports-minded group.

There are water sports in the Yarkon River near Tel Aviv. There the children row and sail and swim. Football (soccer to you), tennis, basketball, hockey, and cricket are popular with boys and girls and grownups. Small children like to roll marbles.

The children also love their puppet shows. One of these shows tells the old tale of King Boor who rules in the Negev. He has imprisoned water. Finally a group of dwarfs and children come to the rescue of the prisoner and let the water out.

The children also like parties. The most important party for a boy is at the time of his *bar-mitzvah*, and for a girl at *bat-mitzvah*. This party is held on the day a child becomes a member of a synagogue. Girls can join at twelve, but boys must wait until they are thirteen. Often there are two parties on this happy day — one in school and one at home.

When boys and girls are fourteen, they can join Godna — an organization something like our Scouts, except that it includes military training. This training is necessary in a country which never knows when it may be attacked.

In spite of danger, Israelis are a merry-hearted people. They love music. It is said that Israel's chief exports are oranges and pianists. You hear people practicing instruments everywhere in Israel. In a ground-floor apartment a violin teacher may be giving lessons, while his wife practices the saxophone in another room. On the floor above there may be a piano player. Above him is a singer. On the top floor are a baby and a cat. Altogether this makes a kind of orchestra, but the music is by no means as beautiful as that of the Israel Philharmonic Symphony Orchestra. It is known all over the world for its wonderful playing. The Philharmonic has played several times in the United States with great success.

The people love dancing too. From the many nations they have brought their folk dances to the new state. Everybody dances the national dance, which is called the *hora*. They dance it till they fall to the ground exhausted, laughing for joy and gasping for breath at the same time.

As the prophet Isaiah said, "Sing, O heavens, and be joyful, O earth, . . . for the Lord hath comforted his people."

Everybody loves a holiday. The joyous spirit of the new nation shines through all its festivals.

The greatest and happiest of these is the Sabbath itself. The Sabbath begins at sunset on Friday and lasts till sunset on Saturday. It is a time for worship, of course, but it's also a time for sports, and for the family to be together. On the Sabbath, families eat food that makes the mouth water, even if they have to save up all week to buy it.

The main meal may start with a clove-spiced fruit soup, made of berries with sour cream, sugar, and lemon juice. Next may come chicken, crisp salad, and almond pudding. Then there is always the Sabbath loaf of bread, or *challa*. This is rich and fluffy, with eggs and sugar added to the dough, and maybe a pinch of saffron. The dough is braided into a fat, humpy loaf, and sometimes baked with poppy seeds on top.

The people are also very fond of *lebben*. These are curds made from sour milk and whipped smooth — often with sugar and strawberries added.

Cholent, the Israelis say, has the taste of paradise. Cholent is beef cooked with onions and other vegetables. It is often baked overnight in the neighborhood baker's oven.

Israel families can choose from many kinds of food, because people from all over have brought their native recipes. From other

Middle Eastern countries, they can choose *shashlik,* chunks of lamb, charcoal-broiled on long skewers. They can choose sesame seed paste from the Orient. Israelis mix it with garlic, parsley, and lemon juice. It tastes extra good with shellfish from the Mediterranean.

And so much fruit! Besides oranges and grapefruit, there are figs and grapes, pomegranates and apples, watermelons and plums. Then there is a vegetable which is an American favorite. Israeli call it *tiras ham.* It's corn on the cob. Children buy it from street-corner vendors. The vendors pop the ears into pots of boiling water. The children wait a minute or two for theirs to cook. Then the vendor hands it to them with the cornhusks for napkins. Away the children go, munching happily. Or perhaps they choose *felafel* — the hot dog of Israel. Made of ground chick-peas, it is served with a vegetable relish between round slices of *pitta,* a thin Oriental bread.

But even though weekday food has great variety, the Sabbath meal is best. On the Sabbath people greet each other by saying *"Shabbat shalom,"* "Sabbath peace." Other days they just say plain "Shalom." Like the Sabbath, many of the Israel festivals are religious holidays, but that doesn't mean that they are days for long faces.

Purim is an example of how gay they can be. It is a day of laughter, dancing, feasting, and hilarious fun. A long time ago, when the people of Israel were living in captivity in Babylonia, a very cruel ruler, named Haman, planned to kill them. A Hebrew maiden, named Esther, pleaded with the ruler and saved her people. Purim celebrates her success. Children love the plump triangular cookies called "ears of Haman" that are baked for this occasion. The cookies are stuffed with jam or fruit and honey.

Today the Purim celebration is something like our Halloween. Boys and girls wear masks. They sing comic songs and people sometimes give them pennies. Grownups, too, dress up in funny clothes. There are parades with floats. You see Noah pass by with his family and his animals. Next comes Joshua with seven priests blowing trumpets, then David and the giant Goliath. There are Jonah and the whale, Solomon and his many wives. Purim is the most exciting holiday in the whole year for children.

Like Purim, the Passover is a celebration of deliverance. Long ago, when the Hebrews were slaves in Egypt, God punished the Egyptian masters for their cruelty. He brought disaster after disaster down upon them. At last the Angel of Death passed over the land. When he passed over the houses of the Hebrews he spared them. This is where the word "Passover" comes from. But the angel killed the first-born sons in all the Egyptian families, including the son of Pharaoh, the ruler. Pharaoh was so stricken that he let the Hebrews escape. So the Israelis are thankful at Passover time.

The holiday begins with a feast called the Seder. There is always delicious food to eat, and everything that is done during the meal has a meaning. At one time *abba,* the father, hides a piece of unleavened bread, called a *matza*. When the children of Israel were leaving Egypt, they were in such a hurry that they couldn't wait for the yeast to make their bread rise. Today, at Passover time, Jews always use unleavened bread, which is bread made without yeast.

You can buy many kinds of *matzoth,* which is the plural of matza, at grocery stores in the United States. Matzoth are very good with butter or honey — or both.

The matza the father hides is called the *aphikomen,* or dessert, since it it eaten at the very end of the meal. The children are supposed to discover where the father hides it, and steal it. Abba doesn't notice it is gone until the end of the meal. Then he doesn't know what to do, as the meal cannot end until the matza is eaten. Finally he has to offer a reward to the children to get it back again.

During the meal the youngest child asks questions about the meaning of Passover. The first question is, "Why is this night different from all other nights?" Then abba tells again the story of the Hebrews' deliverance from the Pharaoh of Egypt.

There are two very solemn holidays in Israel. They are called High Holy Days. One is Yom Kippur, the Day of Atonement. On this day people are supposed to be sorry for their sins. Everyone fasts, except sick people and boys and girls like you.

The other High Holy Day is Rosh Hashana, the beginning of the religious year. The Bible calls it the Day of the Sounding of the Ram's Horn, and in the morning someone blows a loud blast on the *shofar,* which is made from a ram's horn.

Besides Rosh Hashana, there is also a New Year of the Trees. This holiday comes in the spring. In the old days parents planted a tree when a child was born: a cedar for a boy, a cypress for a girl.

As the children grew up, they took care of their trees. Then, when they got married, a branch from the groom's tree and a branch from the bride's tree were used for decorations. The bride and groom hoped the branches would bring them good luck.

Very early in their lives children learned to love trees. They sang songs about them. Today on the New Year of the Trees they get out their spades and plant little saplings. Then they go home and feast on the fruits that grow from the land.

When fruits and grains are harvested, there are festivals, too. In the spring comes Shavuot. This is the time when wheat and barley are brought in from the fields, and the people give thanks.

The second thanksgiving is another holiday that children love. It comes when the grapes and olives are picked in the fall. It's called Sukkoth. *Sukkoth* means "booths." When the people of Israel, led by Moses, were wandering in the wilderness, they made little shelters to sleep in. Now the people imitate these shelters by building sukkoth of canvas, or wood, or branches. If there's no room in the yard, the family may put them on the roof or on the porch.

Many families live in the booths for eight days. What fun that is for the children! The boys and girls like to sleep outdoors and see the stars peeping through the roofs of their sukkoth.

The last day of this festival is the jolliest. There is a feast in the synagogue, with cakes, and salted fish, nuts and fruit. Then the people go about to visit their friends. They sing and dance and stuff themselves with more food. The whole afternoon is spent frolicking. On the last day of Sukkoth the Torah dance is often performed in the streets. A man carrying the Torah, written on a scroll, dances alone in the center of a circle of other men. Gradually the men in the circle begin to sing and shuffle rhythmically from side to side. Then each moves in to kiss the Torah. Next the solo dancer starts a chant. The chorus answers him. Then the dancer moves back into the circle and another replaces him in the center.

If you were in Jerusalem toward the end of the year, one night you would be startled to see great eight-branched candelabra flaming on the tops of Mount Zion and Mount Herzl. All over the country, wherever you went, you would see candles burning. This is the Festival of Lights. The Israelis call it Hanukka. It is ushered in by a freedom torch relay. The first torch is lit from a bonfire in Modiin, northwest of Jerusalem. Then high-school athletes in towns along the way kindle torches from the one that reaches them. Finally a runner brings the last torch to the home of Israel's President. An honor guard salutes as the President accepts the torch. Hanukka has begun.

In the second century before Jesus was born, the Hebrews recaptured their temple at Jerusalem. It had been taken by the Greeks. Once more the triumphant Hebrews lit the altar lamps that had so long been dark. They had only a few drops of oil, but miraculously, they said, the oil lasted for eight days, until they could get more. This miracle is the origin of Hanukka.

The candelabrum used during the Festival of Lights is called a *menora*. It has eight branches and an extra place in the middle for the *shamash*. The father of the family lights the shamash first and then uses it to light all the other candles. But not all at once. The feast lasts for eight days. On the first night he lights only one candle. Every night after that he lights another, until on the eighth night all the candles are burning. Usually there is a separate menora for each member of the family. On the eighth evening the whole house is aglow with light.

This is the time when everybody plays games: chess and checkers, dominoes and cards. There are riddles and puzzles also, and gifts for the children. Boys and girls spin the little Hanukka top. It's called a *svivon* and has four sides. On the sides are four Hebrew letters, N, G, H and P. They stand for four Hebrew words which mean, "A great miracle happened here." This, of course, refers to the miracle of the oil in the temple.

Hanukka comes around our Christmas time, and Christmas too is celebrated by Christians who live in this land where the first

Christmas took place. In Nazareth, where the Arab people are mostly Christians, Christmas starts with the ringing of church bells. Pilgrims from other countries come to visit churches built on historic sites. The Church of the Annunciation stands over the grotto where the Archangel Gabriel is thought to have told Mary about the coming birth of Jesus. The Church of Saint Joseph rises where it is believed Jesus' home once stood.

You wouldn't think, when you take part in Israel's holidays, that for long centuries tyrants tried hard to wipe out people of Jewish faith. They tried, but never succeeded. Out of long suffering and sorrow have come Israel's courage and belief in the future. There are vigorous days ahead, but Israel looks forward to them. It is a nation of the young-in-heart, even though some of the young-hearted have white hair. Children and grownups together dance the hora in the streets on Independence Day. This springtime holiday is like our Fourth of July. It celebrates Israel's birth.

Since its birthday in 1948, the new state has already accomplished what it took some nations centuries to do. First, Israel founded a democratic government, with a congress elected by the people. The congress is called a *knesset*. It in turn elects a president. He appoints the prime minister. Israelis didn't wait to make a constitution before they built their government. The constitution is still being made. Meanwhile the people's right to freedom is guaranteed by laws, and the country has become a member of the United Nations.

There are three times as many people in the country today as when it first became a state. The people are farming three times as much land. They have irrigated this land and planted 30,000,000 new trees. They have built factories which produce almost a billion dollars' worth of goods. They have built ships to take these goods to other lands. When the nation was born, it owned only four little ships. Now it owns more than ten times as many big ones.

These ships sail to other countries, laden with made-in-Israel products which range from razor blades to raincoats. The biggest shiploads are citrus fruits, olive and vegetable oils, automobile tires, cement, potash, drugs, yarns, and diamonds. Ships sailing home into the ports of Haifa, Tel-Aviv, and Eilat are weighed down with tools for making still more goods to be used at home and sold abroad.

It is hard work to make the land produce. Ask the pioneers in the Negev. At the beginning there was nothing there but sand. It was blistering hot — 115 degrees in the shade. And mostly, the people had to work in the sun. After several years of backbreaking toil the land began to bear melons and tomatoes, plums and dates. One of the women who lived through these tough years said: "I tell you, when I heard the chirp of the first bird on our farm, I cried like a child for joy!"

Israel dreams of a brighter future when the birds will be singing all over barren deserts and stony hillsides. The people look to scientists to make this dream come true. They want to sweeten the waters of the Mediterranean and carry them to the farms everywhere. They want to harness the energy of the sun and use the power for factories. They want to be a blessing, not just to themselves, but to all the world.

The ancient land of Israel is young again!

HISTORY

1800–960 B.C. — Tribal civilization ruled by patriarchs. Captivity of the Jews in Egypt, their escape with Moses and Joshua; the founding of a Jewish kingdom with its capital in Jerusalem. Reign of the great kings: Saul, David, Solomon. Also the era of the great prophets of the Old Testament.

930 B.C. — Division of the kingdom into Judah and Israel.

721–424 B.C. — Conquest of Israel by the Assyrians and of Judah by the Babylonians. Disappearance of the Judeans; Israelites taken to Babylon, return to their homeland after two generations of captivity.

424–63 B.C. — The kingdom ruled by Persia, then conquered by Alexander, finally annexed by the Roman Empire.

4 B.C.–29 A.D. — Birth, Ministry and Crucifixion of Jesus Christ.

395–638 — Palestine under the rule of various Middle Eastern and Arab empires. Turkish rule takes over.

1096–1270 — The crusades.

1799 — Napoleonic invasion.

1917 — Beginning of British occupation.

1922 — League of Nations makes the country a British mandate.

1947 — United Nations decides to divide the country into an Arab and a Jewish State.

1948 — Republic of Israel proclaimed. British leave. Arabs attack.

1949 — Armistice agreements signed with Arab states, but no real peace attained.

1950 — Mass migrations of Jewish people from 70 other countries begin.

1951–1960 — Rapid progress in economic and agricultural development, education, health, housing.

Present — Israel expands agriculture, industry, transportation, schools; continues to defend her independence.

SAY IT IN HEBREW

shalom (shah-*lom*) — HELLO (also GOOD-BYE)

bevakashah (beh-vah-kah-shah) — PLEASE

toda (toh-*dah*) — THANK YOU

Anakhu haverim (Ah-nahkh-nu hah-veh-reem) — WE ARE FRIENDS.

Yisrael he eretz mahlhivah. (Issrah-ell hee eh-rets mahl-hee-vah.) — ISRAEL IS AN
EXCITING COUNTRY.

Haisraelim motza'am me shev' eem aratzot shonot. (Hah-iss-rah-ell-im moh-tsah-
ahm mee sheev-eem ah-rah-tsot shoh-note.) — THE PEOPLE OF ISRAEL COME
FROM SEVENTY OTHER COUNTRIES.

B'yahad, ha'anashim bonim moledet hadashah. (Bay-yah-khad hah-ah-nah-sheem
boh-neem moh-led-det hah-dah-shah.) TOGETHER, THE PEOPLE ARE BUILDING A
NEW NATION.

Hamoledet ha'hadashah he gam eretz ha'tnakh. (Hah-moh-leh-dett hah-hah-dah-
shah hee gahm eh-rets hat-nokh.) — THE LAND OF THE NEW NATION IS ALSO
THE OLD LAND OF THE BIBLE.

K'mo ba'tnakh, eer habeerah he Yerushalayim. (Kih-moh bat-nokh eer hah-bee-rah
hee Yeh-roo-shah-lah-eem.) — AS IN THE BIBLE, THE CAPITAL IS JERUSALEM.

*(Where no accents are used, syllables have equal stress. Accents are indicated by
italics.)*

HOW TO PRONOUNCE FOREIGN WORDS IN THIS BOOK

Word	Pronunciation	Word	Pronunciation
abba	*ah*-bah	Ladino	Lah-*dee*-noh
Aden	*Ah*-den	Lod	Ludh
alef	*ah*-lef	Malabar	*Mal*-a-bar
aphikomen	ah-*fee*-koh-men	Mandelbaum	*Man*-dell-bowm
Baal	Bahl	matza	mah-*tsah*
bar-mitzvah	bar-mits-*vah*	matzoth	mah-*tsot*
bat-mitzvah	bott-mits-*vah*	menora	men-oh-*rah*
beit	bayt	Mohammedan	Mo-*ham*-e-dan
bougainvillaea	*boo*-gan-vill-ya	muezzin	moo-eh-*tseen*
caftan	*cahf*-tan	Negev	*Neh*-gehv
carob	*keh*-rub	Purim	Poo-*reem*
challa	*khah*-lah	Rosh Hashana	Rosh *Hash*-ah-*nah*
cholent	*choh*-lent	sabra	*sah*-brah
daganya	dah-*gahn*-ya	Scopus	*Skoh*-puss
Eilat	*ay*-latt	Seder	*Seh*-duh
El Al	ell ahl	Shabbat shalom	*Sha*-bott *shah*-lom
Gaza	*Gah*-za	shamash	*shah*-mahsh
Godna	god-*nah*	shashlik	shash-*lik*
Haifa	Hye-*fah*	Shavuot	shah-voo-*ut*
Herzl	*Hair*-tsl	sherut	shay-*root*
Hindustani	Hin-du-*stahn*-ee	Sukkoth	*Soo*-cuht
Iraq	*Ihr*-ak	svivon	*svee*-von
Israeli	Iz-*rail*-ee	Tel-Aviv	Tell-ah-*veev*
Jaffa	*Yah*-fah	tiras ham	tee-ras *khom*
Judaism	*Jou*-da-ism	Torah	Tor-*ah*
khamsin	k-hahm-*seen*	trempestim	trehm-*pes*-tim
kibbutz	kih-*boots*	ulpanim	ool-pah-*neem*
kibbutzim	kih-boots-*eem*	Via Dolorosa	*Vee*-a *Dole*-o-rose-a
Kinereth	kee-*neh*-ret	Yemen	*Yeh*-men
knesset	k-*ness*-et	Yom Kippur	Yahm Kee-*poor*

63

INDEX